TABLE OF CONTENTS

Page

ACRONYMS

CRS   Congressional Research Service

GSPC   Group for Preaching Combat

GWOT   Global War on Terrorism

NMSP-WOT   National Military Strategic Policy for the War on Terrorism

NGOs   Nongovernmental Organizations

PSI   Pan Sahel Initiative

US   United States

WAMY   World Assembly of Muslim Youth

CHAPTER 1

INTRODUCTION

The Global War on Terrorism (GWOT) requires the United States (US)

government to be engaged in numerous countries and regions around the world, closely

working with the host nations helping to root out terrorists and the causes of terrorism. To

effectively execute this GWOT plan, the US must have the foresight to identify problem

countries before they become safe havens for Islamic extremists. Once Islamic extremists

become entrenched in a country, they have the capability of changing the social dynamics

of that country in a way that makes rooting them out much more costly (Whitehouse

2003).

The Congressional Research Service (CRS) is the public policy research arm of

the US Congress. As a legislative branch agency within the Library of Congress, CRS

works exclusively and directly for members of Congress and their committees and staffs

on a confidential, nonpartisan basis (Congressional Research Service 2006). The research

conducted by this organization impacts US legislative decisions and ultimately US

foreign policy.

In 2004 the CRS produced a report titled *Removing Terrorist Sanctuaries: The*

9/11 Commission Recommendations and U.S. Policy. This 9/11 Commission

Recommendations and US Policy report on Safe Havens and Sanctuaries did not identify

Nigeria as a country requiring "immediate concern." "While Nigeria could potentially

provide sanctuary for terrorists, at present such an outcome appears to be only a

theoretical possibility" (Miko 2004, 20). A review of news sources and informal

1

discussions with US officials indicates that there appear to be few "overt" or apparent indications that there is a current or immediate threat of an international presence in the Mano River Basin countries of Sierra Leone, Liberia, and Guinea, in addition to Nigeria. "While Nigeria has a large Muslim population that includes some radical elements and supporters of Salafist-oriented theologies, as well as numerous self professed admirers of Osama bin Laden, religious linked threats to Nigerian national security have primarily taken the form of recurrent Muslim-Christian violence in central and northern Nigeria and in the commercial capital, Lagos" (Miko 2004, 20, 22). Attacks on US soldiers in Somalia and the bombings of the US embassies in Kenya and Tanzania have been linked to Islamic extremists operating out of Africa. This author's own experience in northern Cameroon and Mali led him to the conclusion that the region is susceptible to the influence of Islamic extremists. The lawlessness, poverty, porous borders, and existence of a strong Muslim tradition in northern Nigeria seemed to confirm this assumption. The ambiguity in the 11 September Report on Terrorist Sanctuaries and Safe Havens indicates a lack of an acute understanding of the realities of West Africa, specifically Nigeria, and a poor understanding of how to wage a global counterinsurgency. The proposed primary research question asks: Is Nigeria operating as an Islamic extremist safe haven?

In order to answer this question the following questions must be researched: What are overt indicators of Islamic extremism? Are there endemic characteristics in Nigeria that make it a place where Islamic extremists can be successful?

Assumptions

Indicators of Islamic extremism can be gathered and identified through unclassified research. The author assumes a minimal level of understanding of Islam from the reader.

Limitations

The research will only use unclassified sources. Due to time and financial constraints, this author was unable to travel to Nigeria. A more complete study would require a visit to northern Nigeria.

Delimitations

The research will focus on Sunni Islam as a vehicle for Islamic extremism. The author is aware of the US State Department's classification of Hizballah. The author researched authors, such as Douglas Farah, who believe that on a tactical and operational level, in Africa, Hizballah and Al Qaeda may be cooperating in West Africa. There is credible open-source evidence that suggest this cooperation continues today. The Lebanese diaspora has great influence in West Africa. However, researching how Hizballah interacts with Al Qaeda Islamic extremists is outside the scope of this paper.

"International terrorism requires two additional factors: a mobilizing, unifying idea, such as that offered by Islamic fundamentalism; and appropriate agitators, who abuse this idea in order to organize a powerful terrorist force against a common external enemy" (Mair 2003, 1). The US is currently at war with a global Islamic extremist insurgency. In order to combat this threat, it is necessary to have a strategy that addresses all aspects of the threat. A successful counterinsurgency strategy involves cooperation

3

and interaction with nations where Islamic extremist insurgents are attempting to gain a foothold. Historical failures in counterinsurgency operations usually involve, in some degree, the inability of the counterinsurgency force to deny the enemy a safe haven or sanctuary. The advantage of a sanctuary or safe haven to an insurgency has been well researched and documented (Joint Chiefs of Staff 2006, 15). Experts agree on the necessity of safe havens and sanctuaries for the success of insurgency operations. However, at present there appears to be a lack of knowledge and understanding by US policy makers of what Islamic extremist insurgents require of a region in order for it to function as a safe haven. This lack of understanding and knowledge of Islamic extremism creates ambiguity and confusion, leading to a disjointed and uncoordinated response to the Islamic extremist threat.

Initial research uncovered indicators of Islamic extremism in the Almajiri Heritage schools in Nigeria. Almajiri Heritage schools are equivalent to Madrassas in Central Asia. These schools represent the traditional Islamic education system transported from Arabia. "The Almajiri Heritage system contains four important features that make it ideal for exploitation by an extremist movement. First, it involves children being relocated--separated from their village family and friends to the guardianship of Mallams in towns. Second, it is restricted almost exclusively to boys. Third, the curriculum of the schools is concerned primarily with teaching the sixty chapters of the Koran by rote memorization. Fourth, each school serves 25 to 500, from the ages 6 to 25. These schools are largely autonomous from government oversight" (Awofeso et al. 2003, 314). The ramifications of this type of education system in a predominately Muslim region of Nigeria will be examined to see the connection these schools may or may not have for the expansion of international Islamic extremism.

Islamic extremists search for opportunities and unique advantages in many regions of the world. Islamic extremists in Nigeria can use cash to bribe government leaders and leverage organized crime to their advantage. Organized crime in Nigeria, combined with the endemic political corruption, may be attractive to Islamic extremists. Nigeria is recognized as a major hub of criminal activity, including narcotics trafficking, illicit financial transactions, and street crime. Nigerian drug traffickers operate worldwide. The country itself serves as an interim destination for heroin and cocaine bound for East Asia, Europe, and North America. To what extent the Islamic extremists have the capability to leverage this organized criminal network to facilitate their operations will be further examined. There is speculation that some branches of the Islamic extremist organization utilize illegal narcotics trafficking to fund terrorist operations. The nexus between organized crime and Islamic extremism is a field that has received attention over the last four years. Studying the current literature on this subject may point to indicators of a partnership of convenience between organized criminals in Nigeria and Islamic extremists (Chalk 2003, 1).

A preponderance of evidence points to the fact that Al Qaeda has been fostering Islamic extremism around the globe in an attempt to build an Islamic army. In building this Islamic army, "Al Qaeda enlisted groups from Saudi Arabia, Egypt, Jordan, Lebanon, Iran Al Qaeda, Oman, Algeria, Libya, Tunisia, Morocco, Somalia, and Eritrea. The links between Al Qaeda and these countries is well established. Moreover, Al Qaeda has also established cooperative but less formal relationships with other extremist groups from these same countries, including the African states of Chad, Mali, Niger, Nigeria, and Uganda, and from the Southeast Asian states of Burma, Thailand, Malaysia, and Indonesia. The groundwork for an insurgency has been laid" (Miko 2004, 58). To what extent these Islamic extremists have successfully initiated and established a safe haven in Nigeria will be examined.

Terms of Reference

Basic concepts about the subject are explained below. Since 11 September 2001, the US government has made several important assumptions about the global Islamic extremist. As an introduction to this chapter it is necessary to describe important terms as they apply to the research questions. The terms below are defined in the context of Islamic extremism. Islam is a religion with many different interpretations. Islamic extremists use Islam as a justification for their actions; thus, understanding how Islamic extremists interpret Islam is important.

Dawa. The Islamization of the Ummah (the global community) through social mobilization in the spirit of Islam. Organizations like the World Assembly of Muslim Youth (WAMY) use Dawa to coordinate the Islamic information operations, working through mosques, universities, schools, and the media to spread the Islamic message. Through Dawa the ground for Jihad is supposed to be prepared (Kurz and Tal 1997).

Islamic extremism or radical Islam. These two terms are interchangeable in this paper. The author will use the term Islamic extremism throughout this thesis, but many articles and books use the term radical Islam. They both have the same meaning. The purpose of Islamic extremism is to eliminate all the gods and replace them with Allah. In order to do this, Islamic extremists generally believe that it is their holy duty to destroy, either violently or through coercion, regimes in all countries so that they pay tribute to the Muslims and become subservient and humiliated (Mazel 2005, 1). President Bush in his January 2006 State of the Union address used radical Islam in characterizing the enemy. "No one can deny the success of freedom, but some men rage and fight against it. And one of the main sources of reaction and opposition is radical Islam--the perversion by a few of a noble faith into an ideology of terror and death" (The White House 2006).

Islamic extremist macro-organizational structure. "In 1998 Al Qaeda was reorganized into four distinct but interlinked entities. The first was a pyramidal structure to facilitate strategic and tactical direction; the second was a global terrorist network; the third was a base force for guerrilla warfare inside Afghanistan; and the fourth was a loose coalition of transnational terrorist and guerrilla groups" (Gunaratna 2002, 76). Since the 11 September attacks on the US and the subsequent US global response, particularly in Afghanistan, the US has forced the Islamic extremists into an extremely clandestine organization (Gunaratna 2002, 78).

Islamic extremist strategic goals. Islamic extremist design is to wage a global insurgency to overthrow governments deemed apostate. The strategic vision of the Islamic extremist global insurgency is to undermine Western influence, redefine the global balance of power, and establish a global pan-Islamist caliphate (Joint Chiefs of Staff 2006, 11). Islamic extremists broadly see the world divided into two houses: The House of Islam (Dar al-Islam), in which the Muslims rule through Islamic law, and the House of War (Dar al Harb), the rest of the world, which is ruled by infidels. The Islamic extremist belief is that Jihad will slowly force the world either to adopt the Muslim faith, succumb to Muslim rule, or die fighting (Harmony Database 2006).

7

Islamic spelling. In transliterating Islamic text into English, words are often spelled phonetically. The result is words such as Sharia, Sha'ria, al Qead, Al Qa'ida are spelled many different ways. The author attempts to stay consistent. However when he used direct quotes he maintained the spelling used by the cited author.

Jihad. The term "Jihad" is a very controversial term. It has very different meanings to different people. For the purpose of this thesis, the term Jihad is defined using Islamic extremist interpretation of this term.

> The ideology, strategy, and tactics of jihad have constituted throughout history a fundamental part of Islamic jurisprudence and literature, since it is through jihad that the Islamic community developed and expanded. Muslim theologians explained that jihad is a collective religious duty binding the entire Muslim community and each individual in certain situations and circumstances. The collective effort can be pursued by military means or peaceful methods-- propaganda, speech, or subversive activities--within a non-Muslim nation. The "enemies" are those who oppose the establishment of Islamic law or its spread, mission, or sovereignty over their lands. (Bat Ye'or 2005, 32)

"Al Qaeda: Is an Islamic Group, its only mission is Jihad; because Jihad is one of the basic purposes for which Al Qaeda personnel come together. In addition, they perform other Islamic duties if possible. Jihad will take precedence over other duties in case of interference. The goal of Al Qaeda is the victory of the mighty religion of Allah, the establishment of an Islamic Regime and the restoration of the Islamic Caliphate, God willing" (Harmony Database 2006).

Madrassas. An Islamic education system that serves as a recruitment, indoctrination, and training mechanism for Islamic extremists to promulgate Islamic extremist ideology.

Nonphysical safe haven (virtual safe haven). Terrorist groups are increasingly using new information technology and the internet to formulate plans, raise funds, spread propaganda, and engage in secure communications. The term nonphysical safe haven or virtual safe haven refers to those capabilities exploited through cyber tactics, techniques, and practices of the Islamic extremist.

Sharia law. Broadly defined, Sharia law is a combination of constitutional law and political philosophy. Islam does not distinguish between church and state. Extreme Islam believes God is the sole sovereign and the only source of law. This law is encompassed in the Koran (Lewis 2003, 7).

Sunnah. "The habits and religious practice of the Prophet Muhammad, which were recorded for posterity by his companions and family and are regarded as the ideal Islamic norm. They have thus been enshrined in Islamic law, so that Muslims can approximate closely to the archetypal figure of the Prophet, in his perfect surrender to (Islam) God" (Armstrong 2002, 206).

The Koran (Qur'an). "The Qur'an, for Muslims, is a single book promulgated at one time by one man, the Prophet Muhammad. After a lively debate in the first centuries of Islam, the doctrine was adopted that the Qur'an itself is uncreated and eternal, divine and immutable" (Lewis 2004, 8). Islamic extremists believe Muhammad abolished all prophets before him and to follow any teaching other than Muhammad's is unjustified and satanic (Trifkovic 2002, 147).

The Pan Sahel Initiative (PSI). PSI initiated in 2004, is a US-State-Department-funded program in the northern African countries of Mali, Mauritania, Niger, and Chad, designed to enhance border capabilities throughout the region against arms smuggling, drug trafficking, and the movement of transnational terrorists (globalsecurity.org 2006).

Ummah. The global Muslim community, as defined by Islamic extremists.

9

CHAPTER 2

LITERATURE REVIEW

The study of Islamic extremism has dynamic, constantly changing qualities, especially as it relates to Nigeria. The majority of reviewed literature supports the hypothesis of Nigeria as a possible Islamic safe haven. There were five major concepts explored in the review of literature of Islamic extremism: ideology, origin of Islamic extremism, key influential leaders, Sharia law, and characteristics of Muslims in Nigeria. In order to gain the clearest picture in the field of Islamic extremism, the following unclassified sources were used: professional journals, magazines, books by respected authors who are recognized as experts in the field, and unclassified open source websites.

"Modern interpretations of Islamic teachings and its culture have produced a specific ideology of extremism that is in direct conflict with democratic philosophy of the US and the Western world" (Huntington 1996, 213.). This section first examines the development of Islamic extremist ideology, the emergence of Islamic extremism in Nigeria, and events in and characteristics of Nigeria that make it an ideal country for establishing Islamic extremist safe havens, where Islamic extremists can entice potential recruits, raise money and launder it, maintain freedom of movement for leadership and command and control, and launch attacks against US and Western interests.

Islamic teaching and its culture have produced the ideology against which the US is currently at war. Therefore, it is a requirement to examine Islam and identify what it is about Islam that produces this ideology. The literature researched critically analyzed Islam for characteristics that lead to extremism.

Karen Armstrong's works include *A History of God*, 1993; *The Battle for God*, 2000; and *Islam: A Short History*, 2000. Taken together these books are a comprehensive work on Islam and Christianity and how they interact with one another. The author found Armstrong's work on the matter of Islam and extremism very informative.

Armstrong identifies the origins of modern Islamic extremism. She differentiates fundamentalism from mainstream Islam, and separates Sunni extremism from Shiite extremism. Her work clearly identifies the teachings and ideology behind the modern Islamic extremist movement. For example, there exists a "doctrinal" linkage to Al Zawahiri's and Osama bin Laden's strategic message. The linkage unveils itself in similar concepts, relations of concepts, and methods.

Samuel Huntington takes a macro-level look at Islam and its relationship to the West. He sees Islam as a culture that in its entirety is diametrically opposed to Western individualism and secular government. His work *Clash of Civilizations*, published in 1996, has been called seminal by some of the most respected men in international affairs and political science. He clearly identifies endemic characteristics in Islamic and Western societies that cause conflict and "war." History has shown that the West and Islam are not able to coexist without war and conflict.

> The relations between Islam and Christianity, both Orthodox and Western, have often been stormy. Each has been the other's other. The twentieth-century conflict between liberal democracy and Marxist-Leninism is only a fleeting and superficial historical phenomenon compared to the continuing and deeply conflictual relations between Islam and Christianity. The causes of this ongoing pattern of conflict lie not in transitory phenomenon such as twelfth-century Christian passion or twentieth-century Muslim fundamentalism. They flow from the nature of the two religions (Christianity and Islam) and the civilizations based on them. (Huntington 1996, 209-218)

Huntington writes about a natural conflict between Islam and the West. Islam has not gone through a Reformation; the Koran dictates that Muslims must be governed by Sharia law. There is no difference between religion and state government. He believes there is a fundamental conflict between Christianity and Islam. Both religions claim to be the one true faith. He believes that the fundamental beliefs of Christianity and Islam have led to centuries of conflict and struggle between the two faiths. This "clash" of two civilizations, as he calls it, is inevitable (Huntington 1996, 210-212).

Huntington rightly illustrates the historical and future conflict between Islam and Christianity or the West. He does not differentiate between Islamic extremism and moderate Islam. He states that American leaders allege that the Muslims involved in the quasi-war are a small minority whose use of violence is rejected by the great majority of moderate Muslims. This may be true, but evidence to support it is lacking. According to Huntington, the underlying problem for the West is not Islamic fundamentalism. It is that Islam is a different civilizations whose adherents are convinced of the superiority of their culture and are obsessed with the inferiority of their power. These are the basic ingredients that fuel conflict between Islam and the West (Huntington 1996, 217-218).

Huntington's explanation of the endemic causes of conflict between the West and Islam lends credibility to the term "Islamic extremist." His classification of Islam has drawn criticism from scholars, such as John L. Esposito, who think Huntington paints too negative picture of the religion of Islam. However, Huntington's work is important because it illustrates how Islam as a religion is a fundamental unifying characteristic of the enemy the US faces.

Samuel Huntington's discussion on "cleft" countries is an important concept for this research. He defines cleft countries as countries where large groups belong to different civilizations. "Such divisions and the tensions that go with them often develop when a majority group belonging to one civilization attempts to define the state as its political instrument and to make its language, religion, and symbols those of the state." He further warns that cleft countries that territorially bestride the fault lines between civilizations face particular problems maintaining their unity. In Sudan, civil war has gone on for decades between Muslims in the North and Christians in the South. Nigeria's geographical location on the buffer zone between Christian Sub-Saharan Africa and the Muslim-dominated Pan-Sahel makes it a cleft country. The cleft concept is important to understand because the Islamic extremists prefer to operate in cleft regions of the world (Huntington 1996, 137).

A review of the strategic guidance issued by key communicators within the Islamic extremist movement was conducted. Open-source reporting from the Foreign Broadcast Information Service and Congressional Reports identifies consistencies in the Islamic extremist strategic message. Islamic extremists detail exactly what they are going to do. They have limited capability to operate in what the military would refer to as a "secret" closed system. Therefore, everything they do and say should be taken at face value. As a matter of necessity, Islamic extremists must spread their extremist message in the open source environment; otherwise, their targeted audience would not receive the message.

In a CRS report, Christopher M. Blanchard reviews Al Qaeda's use of public statements from the mid-1990s to the present and analyzes the evolving ideological and political content of those statements. The Islamic extremists who follow the guidance of Osama bin Laden and his Al Qaeda association have a very clear strategic message for the Muslim community writ large. The three foundations, as outlined by Al Zawahiri (the number two leader in Al Qaeda), are as follows: most importantly, the cornerstone of Al Qaeda's religious and political rhetoric has remained consistent. Muslims should view themselves as a single nation and unite to resist anti-Islamic aggression on the basis of obligatory defensive Jihad. Non-Islamic government is unacceptable, and Muslims should join Al Qaeda and other sympathetic groups and movements in opposing those seeking to establish secular democratic governments or maintain existing governments deemed to be insufficiently Islamic (Blanchard 2005, 8).

"Stealing Al-Qa'ida's Playbook," published by the Counter Terrorism Center at West Point in February 2006, is a short but very important article. It recognizes that the Islamic extremist message and strategic plan are available for all those who wish to read them. The article claims that academia and Western intelligence analysis have done a poor job in reading open-source documents that describe in detail what the strategic thinkers within the Islamic extremist core group are thinking. This report looks at the strategic communication of Al Qaeda.

Documents from the Harmony Database provided by the Counter Terrorism Center have just been made public. The Counter Terrorism Center is an excellent unclassified resource for research into Islamic extremism. Two documents used for background information were: "Al-Qa'ida Goals and Structure" and "Al-Qa'ida Constitutional Charter." These documents provide valuable insight into the strategic thinking at the highest level of the Al Qaeda movement. The consistency in the themes, which the Islamic extremists have maintained throughout their modern history are very apparent. The documents indicate a very well coordinated thoughtfully planned "strategic communication" agenda which has stayed on message throughout the existence of the organization now referred to as Al Qaeda. It is very clear after reading through this constitutional charter that their interpretation of Islam is the driving force behind their strategic message.

Paul Marshall, a senior fellow at Freedom House's Center for Religious Freedom, has written extensively about Sharia law. Understanding that the linkage between government and religion is fused with the implementation of Sharia law helps one recognize overt indicators of Islamic extremism. As a general rule, where one finds Islamic extremism one also finds an extreme form of Sharia law.

Paul Marshall identifies a moderate movement within the Islamic community and clearly points to indicators that lead to extremism. By characterizing extreme Sharia law, he, by default, recognizes the existence of a moderate or benign form of Islamic governance. This identification of a benign or moderate form of Islam is important when discussing the conflict within Islam. Marshall points to a religious battle between moderate and extreme interpretations of Islam. His analysis is important to this research because it assists in identifying distinct characteristics within the Islamic religion.

Irit Back, who publishes in the Tel Aviv Notes, has studied the progress Osama bin Laden has made in Africa and details the challenges Africa poses to Islamic extremism. The arrival of Islam in sub–Saharan Africa was more gradual and peaceful. The message of a new religion was spread by individual agents, merchants, travelers, and missionaries. Islam was adopted mainly by the ruling elites and did not gain a stronghold

15

with the majority of the African masses. Moreover, Islamization was accompanied by a process of Africanization, that is, the absorption of elements of African religions and traditions.

Islam came to be adopted as a loose form of identity for tribal societies. In other cases, it was the common denominator for subjects of large empires, and it became a basis for social order and political authority. This was the particular case in Northern Nigeria and coastal areas of Kenya. Until the nineteenth century, Islam was closely associated with class and the ruling elite. That began to change with the appearance of the Jihad movement of Uthman dan Fodio (1754-1817), who was one of the most influential Islamic scholars in the history of Islam in West Africa. He was both a Mujahid, fighter for the sake of Islam, and Mujahid reformer of the place that is historically known as the Sokoto Khalifate of West Africa (Islam On-line 2006). This was a militant movement to spread Islam beyond its traditional boundaries, but it also carried a message of social reform that appealed to the alienated masses by stressing education and social welfare. The resurgence of Islamic militancy in northern Nigeria is grounded in Uthman dan Fodio's heritage. Some experts consider Bin Laden to be the contemporary standard-bearer of his legacy in northern Nigeria (Back 2002). The Islamic militancy described in Back's article provides historical context to the political and social role of Islam in Nigeria.

In a paper titled "African Vortex: Islamism in Sub-Saharan Africa," David McCormack, a research associate at the Center for Security Policy in Washington, DC, details the introduction of Islam into Africa and the subsequent influence Saudi Arabia had on the Nigerian Islamic north. McCormack traces Saudi Arabian involvement in

Nigeria, which began in the 1960s. Most importantly, he identifies Sardauna of Sokoto Alhaji Sir Ahmadu Bello, often called the first prime minister of northern Nigeria, and his chief advisor, Alhaji Abubakar Gumi, as prominent Nigerian Muslim leaders who, with the assistance of Riyadh, changed the face of Islam in Nigeria. His work on Islam in Sub-Saharan Africa details Islam in Nigeria and the involvement of Saudi Arabia and the Wahhabist sect of Islam. This linkage between Islam in Nigeria and Saudi Arabia is important for identifying overt indicators associated with Islamic extremism in Northern Nigeria (McCormack 2005, 12).

The US Institute of Peace, Special Report "Political Islam in Sub-Saharan Africa" is an excellent source for understanding Islam in sub-Saharan Africa. Politically Islam has played an important role in the evolution of Nigeria's polity, but it must be assessed in terms of the daunting political and economic challenges facing the country. Northern Nigeria's largely Muslim Hausa-Fulani people have long-standing transnational connections to Middle Eastern centers of learning and West African Sufi brotherhoods. British colonialism bolstered northern Nigeria's control by political Islamists. In exchange for support of British rule, Ahmadu Bello was able to insist on the teaching and practice of Islam in this region. Traditional Islamic clans coalesced into a northern party that effectively excluded Westernized intellectuals and secularized non-Muslims. The resurgence of Islamic fundamentalism in Nigeria following independence was influenced by an infusion of Saudi-educated religious scholars who challenged less austere versions of Africanized Islam.

Niyi Awofeso, J. E. Ritchie, and P. J. Degeling in their article "The Almajiri Heritage and the Threat of Non-State Terrorism in Northern Nigeria--Lessons from

Central Asia and Pakistan" describe similarities between Central Asian Madrassas and the Muslim education system in Nigeria. Their thesis is that this type of education system serves as a potential recruitment and indoctrination mechanism for Islamic extremists to promulgate Islamic extremist ideology. The Aljamiri heritage is, like the Madrassas in Central Asia, a system of Muslim education that dates back several centuries. Given the presence of Islamic extremism in North Africa and the imposition of Sharia law in northern Nigeria since 1999, the authors of this article believe these school systems offer an excellent vehicle to be exploited by Islamic extremists. These schools often educate or, more correctly, indoctrinate their pupils in an extreme form of Islam called Wahhabism. The authors compare the religious schools in Nigeria with those in Central Asia before and during the Soviet communist rule. Drawing on the trajectory of similar educational systems in Central Asia prior to, during, and following Russian communist rule, this article offers reasons for the growing terrorist potential of the Almajiri heritage (Awofeso et al. 2002, 311).

Douglas Farah's detailed analysis of Islamic extremist connections to West Africa provides insight into the elaborate infrastructure set up there by Islamic extremists prior to 11 September. In addition, Farah details a connection between Hizballah and Al Qaeda. Relevant to the thesis question about overt indicators of Islamic extremism in West Africa is the research conducted detailing an extensive Islamic extremist infrastructure established in West Africa prior to 11 September.

Farah's work has challenged the US Government intelligence community on the existence of Islamic extremists operating in West Africa. His book, *Blood From Stones*, gives background to the way in which the enemy has operated for many years in West

Africa. Farah's detailed account of Al Qaeda operations to corner the diamond market in Sierra Leone is instructive. Farah's firsthand experience meeting with rebel leaders in Sierra Leone, including personal dealings with several high ranking Al Qaeda operators, further illustrates how West Africa is being used by the Islamic extremists to further their goals.

Inside Al Qaeda by Rohan Gunaratna offers a comprehensive analysis of the Islamic extremist organization's global architecture. The author depicts an organization, which is run by a core group but maintains the capability to connect to the Muslim on the street. By decentralizing much of their operations the core Arab Islamic extremists are able to influence regions by "franchising" regional Islamic extremism. Relevant to this research is the author's detailed description of how Al Qaeda "franchises" regional Islamic extremist organizations to act on its behalf. This act turns regional threats into international ones, and creates geographical areas where the Islamic extremists maintain freedom of movement and provide support to ongoing and future Islamic extremist organizations. Taken together, both Gunaratna and Farah have contributed immensely to how the US should understand Islamic extremism.

Prepared by Francis T. Miko, a specialist in international relations, *Removing Terrorist Sanctuaries: The 9/11 Commission Recommendations and U.S. Policy* was directed through the 11 September Report. Its purpose was to draft a policy paper identifying and prioritizing actual terrorist sanctuaries and to employ for each a realistic strategy to keep possible terrorists insecure and on the run, using all instruments of national power. This report analyzes US policies targeting terrorist sanctuaries in countries and regions highlighted in the 11 September Commission Recommendations.

Miko's report offers an overview of regions of the world the US government considers sanctuaries. Miko explains characteristics of a safe haven but fails to explain or articulate how the Islamic extremist utilizes or might be identified within the safe haven.

Laremont and Gregorian in an article titled "Political Islam in West Africa" recognize the existence of radical Islam in West Africa. They conclude a major contributing factor to the existence of radical Islam in West Africa is the inability of the respective governments to monitor the political situation within the austere isolated regions of their countries, and the existence of a poverty-stricken population which is susceptible to the "proselytizing and recruitment of radical Muslim elements who draw inspiration from Al Qaeda" (Laremont and Gregorian 2006, 36). This work is important to the research because it recognizes the existence of Islam as a political mechanism within Nigeria. Laremont and Gregorian identify serious threats to US national security as coming from West Africa. Specifically the authors highlight three potential threats: the emergence of Al-Qaeda-associated movements in Nigeria and Niger; the existence of terrorist-financing networks, which are leveraging the unregulated diamond mines in Sierra Leone, Liberia, and Democratic Republic of Congo to fund Islamic extremist operations; and the expansion of Al-Qaeda-associated terrorist movements, such as the Salafist Group for Preaching Combat (GSPC) from southern Algeria, to safe havens into trans-Sahel countries like Mali, northern Niger, and northern Chad. Laremont and Gregorian do not recognize any one country in West Africa as a "safe haven" nor do they link Al-Qaeda-affiliated organizations in West Africa with a wider global Islamic extremist ideology; nonetheless, the article is extremely relevant to the research of Islamic extremism in Africa (Laremont and Gregorian 2006, 1).

Methodology

According to the National Military Strategic Policy for the War on Terrorism (NMSP-WOT), "Ideology is the component most critical to extremist networks and movements and sustains all other capabilities." Islamic extremism ideology is the foundation on which everything is built. The identifiable existence of an Islamic extremist ideology is the first indicator this paper uses to show a country is a safe haven for Islamic extremists. Second, the resources to support this ideology must exist. Resources are defined in the NMSP-WOT as "a person, organization, place, or thing (physical or non-physical) and its attributes." Without the proper resources to support an ideology, that ideology cannot thrive. The third criterion this paper uses to show that a country is a safe haven is the existence of poor government control. Poor government control allows for "entities [groups] outside the law" to "find space in the vacuums left by declining or transitional states" (Shultz et al. 2004, 8).

Islamic extremist ideology creates the conditions for exploitation of the resources, and a weak central government has no capability to stop this. The premise is that if these characteristics exist in any country or region, global Islamic extremist insurgents can potentially use the country or region to promote its extremist ideology and promulgate activities conducive to the organization's goals. In other words, if the fire department is called to put out a fire that means the fire marshal missed his opportunity to identify and clean up combustible trash before it became a problem. Islamic extremist ideology, resources available for exploitation, and a weak central government are the "fire starters" which the marshal should have identified and removed before the building burned down. The purpose of using this particular methodology is to help policy makers better

21

categorize and define characteristics that can point to the existence of Islamic extremism and better coordinate all instruments of national power to clean out the "trash" before it becomes a fire.

CHAPTER 3

ANALYSIS

Introduction

The GWOT is a global war against an ideology that is in direct conflict with Western values. The global nature of this war requires US government resources to be applied in numerous countries and regions around the world in a coordinated manner. To effectively utilize strategic resources the US government must be able to identify characteristics of an Islamic extremist safe haven and identify problem areas before the enemy becomes established in a country or region. A common understanding of the ideology of the enemy, the characteristics or resources the enemy seeks to utilize in a safe haven, and the enabling role a weak central government has in perpetuating the Islamic extremist operations must be established to better coordinate the US federal government response to the global Islamic extremist insurgency.

In the introduction, the author highlighted a CRS report which reflected a poor understanding of the ground truth as it relates to Islamic extremist operations and the functions of safe havens with respect to those operations, specifically within Nigeria. The analysis will show that with a better understanding of the Islamic extremist ideology and an appreciation for what this enemy requires to function, the US government can standardize classifications for a safe haven and apply the full spectrum of its national power to counter the enemy it faces in these safe havens.

In order to prove that Nigeria is being used as an Islamic extremist safe haven, the research will first conduct a historical background analysis of Islamic extremist ideology and define the nature of a safe haven. Understanding the Islamic extremist's ideological evolution is an important aspect in understanding the scope of the threat of Islamic extremism. Islamic extremism has an ideological linage that can be identified and analyzed.

Ideology Background

Islam and Islamic thought can be divided into two major sects: Sunni Islam, the majority sect, and Salafi (Arabic for "predecessors"). Sunni Islam can be further divided into four main schools, or madhabs, of Islamic jurisprudence: Hanafi, Hanbali, Shafi'i, and Maliki. It is important to understand Islamic extremist are not a monolithic movement; however, discussion of the four schools of Sunni Islam are outside the scope of this paper. The Salafi movement, inspired by the thirteenth-century Syrian theologian Ibn Taymiya, rejects many mainstream Islamic traditions and considers its views to be the "pure" Islam. Within the Salafi movement, there exists a more extreme Wahhabi sect, named after the eighteenth-century thinker Muhammad ibn Abd al-Wahhab. Terrorist organizations such as al-Qaeda, Hamas, Islamic Jihad, Hizb ut-Tahrir, Tablighi Jam'aat, and the Muslim Brotherhood follow Wahhab. They have distorted mainstream, classical Islamic traditions for narrowly political ends (Baran 2005).

A very important part of understanding the ideology of Islam is recognizing that it does not differentiate between church and state. The Koran dictates governance through Sharia law. Sharia law presupposes and demands the existence of an Islamic state as an executor to enforce the law. To be legitimate, all political power therefore must rest with those who enjoy Allah's authority on the basis of his revealed will sent down through the prophet. Society is regulated by law, and in the Islamic state the source of law is divine. Politics is not part of Islam. Politics is the inherent core of the Islamic imperative of

24

Allah's sovereignty. Sharia is therefore infallible. Sharia applies to all humankind just as the Koran applies to all creation. Any law that is inconsistent or in conflict with it should be null and void, not only to the Muslims, but to all humanity. Jews, Christians, and pagans are subject to Sharia (Trifkovic 2002, 146-147).

Understanding the Koran and the role Sharia law plays in ruling Muslims offers evidence that it can be used as a tool for extremism. Universally those who follow Judeo-Christian traditions, upon which much of Western law is based, would view the former Taliban government or the Saudi Arabian judiciary as extremist. Western culture and society condemn executing women accused of adultery or amputating a criminal's hand for stealing; yet these are two examples of extreme actions dictated by Sharia law. Sharia law is a good indicator of extremist tendencies. How extremists are able to implement their form of Sharia law is a gauge from which one can determine the level of control the Islamic extremists have over the society and its existing culture.

Karen Armstrong's *Battle for God, A History of Fundamentalism* identifies the foundation of modern Islamic extremism ideology. Ideology by definition is a set of beliefs, values, and opinions that shapes the way an individual or a group such as a social class thinks, acts, and understands the world. Armstrong traces modern Islamic extremism back to Abul Ala Mawdudi, founder of Jamaat-I Islami in Pakistan (1903-1979). According to Armstrong, Mawdudi feared the West was growing too strong politically and would destroy Islam. He felt God was the "supreme legislator" and humans "had no right to make up their own laws or take control of their destiny." He felt a ruler who did not govern following the will of God according to the Koran and the Sunnah could not rule over others. Mawdudi suggested an ideology of Islamic liberation through revolutionary means against those who did not follow the Islamic God. He demanded a universal Jihad. His militant ideology shared characteristics of Marxism (Armstrong 2000, 236). Karen Armstrong links Mawdudi to what many scholars consider Sunni fundamentalism.

Mawdudi's teachings inspired the father of modern Islamic extremism, Sayyid Qutb (1906-1966). While imprisoned, Sayyid Qutb came to believe that religious people and secularists could not live together in harmony. He felt secularists lacked anything and everything considered moral and sacred. Qutb "transformed the mythos of Mawdudi into an ideology." He simplified the ideas of Mawdudi and his ideology resulted into a "distorted Islamic vision" (Armstrong 2000, 239).

Karl Sageman, like Karen Armstrong, traces the roots of the current Islamic extremist movement back to Mawdudi and Qutb. Both Mawdudi and Qutb represent primary influential leaders in modern Islamic extremist ideology. Unlike Armstrong, Sageman includes the Sufi and Wahhabist sect as the vanguard sect within the Islamic extremist movement.

Sageman describes Mohamed ibn Abd a-Wahhab (1703-1791) as an Arabian Peninsula preacher who had rejected the depravity of the prevailing popular beliefs and practices of the tribes of the peninsula. He claimed they had reverted to the state of jahilliyya, a state without Islam, and deserved death for abandoning Islam. Mohamed ibn Abd a-Wahhab advocated a strict interpretation of the Koran. His central doctrine was Tawhid, "Unity of God," which preached against false idols, such as saints or shrines. He joined with a local tribal chief, Mohamed ibn Saud, forming a revivalist political movement to purify Islam and fulfill its godly promise. He used jahiliyya as the justification for waging war on fellow Muslims. The Wahhabi-Saudi alliance conquered most of the peninsula by the end of the eighteenth century. It destroyed all the sacred tombs, including the tomb of the Prophet, massacred the Muslims of the Holy Cities, and imposed its own standards on Muslim pilgrims.

Sagemen describes the Islamic extremist terrorist and associates extremist terrorism with the Saudi Arabian Wahhabi and Salafi sect of Islam. The global Salafi Jihad is a worldwide religious revivalist movement with the goal of reestablishing past Muslim glory in a great Islamic state stretching from Morocco to the Philippines, eliminating present national boundaries. It preaches salafiyyah (from salaf, the Arabic word for "ancient one" and referring to the companions of the Prophet Mohammed) and the restoration of authentic Islam, and advocates a strategy of violent Jihad, resulting in an explosion of terror to wipe out what it regards as local political heresy. A global version of this movement advocates the defeat of those preventing the establishment of a true Islamic state, mainly the West (Sagemen 2004, 1). In his book *Understanding Terrorist Networks*, he links the Wahhabi doctrine to the Mawdudi and Qutb. Sayyid Qutb took Wahhab's idea of waging Jihad against apostates and Mawdudi's concept of jahiliyya and combined them, extending ibn abd al Wahhab's ideas even further, thus linking the Salfi or Salafiyya and Wahhabist (Sageman 2004, 9).

Sayyid Qutbs' *Milestones*, published in 1964, linked Salafi and Wahhabi ideology and became the manifesto for the Salafi Jihad. It directly influenced the Egyptian wing of those recognized today as members of the key leadership of Al Qaeda: Ayman al Zawahiri (credited as being the ideological force behind Osama bin Laden), Ali Amin Ali Al Rashidi, and Subhi Muhammad Abu Sitta. This linkage can be identified and analyzed

27

through current Islamic extremist strategic communications (Sageman 2004, 9). For example, Al Qaeda, as did Qutb, believes in an Islamic state governed solely by Sharia law. The goals of bin Laden and Zawahiri are to free the Muslim lands from all who do not believe in their ideologies, and especially from Western influence. Al Zawarhiri goes even further in describing a vision where a relationship exists between Muslims and their ruler that would permit people to choose and criticize their leaders, but also demands that Muslims overthrow those who violate Islamic laws and principles. He identifies a need for a Sharia-based judiciary that states that no one can dispose of the people's rights, except in accordance with this judiciary. In the end Zawahiri and the global Islamic extremists see as their end state a large Caliphate ruled through a strict interpretation of the Koran (Blanchard 2005, 8).

The cornerstone of Al Qaeda's religious and political rhetoric has remained consistent. Muslims should view themselves as a single nation and unite to resist anti-Islamic aggression on the basis of obligatory defensive Jihad. Non-Islamic government is unacceptable, and Muslims should join Al Qaeda and other sympathetic groups and movements in opposing those seeking to establish secular democratic governments or maintain existing governments deemed to be insufficiently Islamic (Blanchard 2005, 8).

The core leadership of the premier Islamic extremist organization in the world clearly uses Islam as the justification for its action and counts on the masses within the Islamic community to carry the fight. Its strategic message has been constant and has not veered from some of the early key communicators such as Qutb. This consistency is value added and has made the spread of their message more effective.

Sageman speaks to the psychological aspects of Islamic extremism. As stated above, he draws a direct linkage from the Salafist ideology to the motivation behind the Islamic extremist movement. He concludes Salafi behavioral prescriptions demand sacrifices for the sake of the group. Becoming a Salafist involves great personal cost, often including rejection by one's former friends, family, or even employer, if they do not approve of the group or its attitudes. Furthermore, Salafi behavior is highly visible. It is a proclamation of one's faith in God. Growing one's beard, dressing like a traditional Muslim, and giving up some of one's pleasures are sacrifices for God and the true community. This distances new devotees from their original network of friends and family, but draws them closer to other Salafists, whose good opinion becomes their only reference (Sageman 2004, 118). In summary, Islamic extremists are "a transnational movement of extremist organizations, networks, and individuals . . . which have in common that they exploit Islam and use terrorism for ideological ends" (Joint Chiefs of Staff 2006, 13).

The Nature of a Safe Haven

In broad terms, a safe haven must have the resources available to "provide the enemy freedom of action to plan, train, rest and conduct operations." Safe havens provide resources in the form of ideological support, financial support, command and control, information operations, people, and freedom of movement. Those using safe havens benefit "when the states grant them access to territory through active support, tacit support, or through a lack of government capability to stop it" (Joint Chiefs of Staff 2006, 15). Safe havens are "distinguished by rugged terrain, poor accessibility . . . and little government presence." The key characteristic is poor government control (Shultz et al. 2004, 8).

An area can be categorized specifically as an Islamic extremist safe haven if it performs those functions the Islamic extremist requires. These are further categorized in the NMSP-WOT into:

> 1. Finance: Extremists fund operations using unofficial banking systems, legitimate businesses, front companies, wealthy backers, state sponsors, NGOs, and organized crime.

> 2. Communication: The ability to receive, store, manipulate, and communicate and or disseminate information is critical for the Islamic extremist. This can and does take advantage of the global information grid, and therefore can be located almost anywhere.

> 3. Movement: Islamic extremists need to move people, things, and ideas around with as little interference as possible from unfavorable governments. This requires couriers, movement corridors and transit points, relative anonymity, organic and commercial transportation, popular support, and illicit and criminal trade mechanisms.

> 4. Intelligence: Islamic extremists perform counterintelligence, apply operations security measures, use denial and deception and exercise great care to determine the loyalty and reliability of members, associates, active supporters, and other affiliates.

> 5. Weapons: Access and the ability to secure weapons and weapon components from the black market with little to no government interference is an important function.

> 6. Personnel: This critical capability incorporates terrorist recruitment, indoctrination, and training of enemy operatives. Extremists use religious facilities, schools, refugee camps, NGOs, and the media as vehicles for recruitment, reinforced by the educational and indoctrination efforts.

> 7. Ideology: The existence of an ideology and a mechanism with which to spread it to the population is a very important indicator of an Islamic extremist presence. (Joint Chiefs of Staff 2006, 15-18)

The 11 September Commission attempts to identify and prioritize actual terrorist sanctuaries. It analyzes US policies targeting terrorist sanctuaries in countries and regions highlighted in the 11 September Commission Recommendations. Within this report, Miko offers a description of the function of terrorist sanctuaries.

> [A] complex international terrorist operation aimed at launching a catastrophic attack cannot be mounted without the time, space, and ability to perform competent planning and staff work; a command structure able to make necessary decisions and possessing the authority and contacts to assemble needed people, money, and materials; opportunity and space to recruit, train, and select operatives with the needed skills and dedications, providing the time and structure required to socialize them into the terrorist cause, judge their trustworthiness, and hone their skills; a logistics network able to securely manage the travel of operatives, move money, and transport resources where they need to go; access, in the case of certain weapons, to the special materials needed for a nuclear, chemical, radiological, or biological attack; reliable communications between coordinators and operatives; and opportunity to test the workability of a plan. (Miko 2004, 1)

Safe havens are one of the most important aspects of the Islamic extremist network (Joint Chiefs of Staff 2006, 15). They offer the Islamic extremist the ability to project power and sustain ideological and operational support.

Physical and nonphysical safe havens require either tacit support of a government or they require that a government lack the ability to stop those functions the Islamic extremist require. Put simply, they require poor government control, which is characterized as a country ruled by self-interested leaders, at all levels of government, who rule over corrupt government. These leaders leverage criminal networks to divide the country's wealth. This undermines and discredits the government and sets the conditions for organized crime. Corruption permeates all facets of law enforcement, to include the national military, which results in lack of authority and respect for these organizations. Poor government control is a condition of a government that is unable to accomplish those function a government is required to do, such as secure borders, distribute wealth, enforce national laws, and regulate commerce (Shultz et al. 2004, 24).

Analysis

After examining the Islamic extremist ideology and defining a safe haven, the research will now show how Nigeria is an Islamic extremist safe haven because certain indicators exist. The following three indicators are the focus of this paper: an Islamic extremist ideology, available resources, and poor government control.

With an understanding of the ideology of the Islamic extremists, one can look at Nigeria's Muslim population and see how historical events there have fueled the Islamic extremists' ideologies to spread. Saudi Arabian Wahhabism has been actively promoted in Nigeria since the 1960s. This sect of Islam has become the most popular sect in Nigeria. Saudi Arabia's wealth from oil has contributed billions of dollars over the last thirty years to funding Wahabism. Saudi Arabian Wahhabist influence in Nigeria can be directly traced through the careers of two Nigerian Muslim leaders: Alahi Sir Ahmadu Bello, the Sardauna of Sokoto, and Alhaji Abubakar Gumi, his chief advisor. Of the two, Abubakar Gumi was more inclined towards Wahabism. Gumi was immersed in Wahabism tradition when he lived several months in the Hija (McCormack 2005, 9).

Despite its spread from the 1960s onward, the extent of Islam's grip on Nigeria became clear only with the country's liberation from military rule in 1999. This event marked a rapid decline in the power of the central government. Now free to implement their program at the state level, Islamists in northern Nigeria embarked on a campaign to transform social and political life to conform to the dictates of radical Wahhabist Islam (McCormack 2005, 10-11).

Along with the political freedom provided by the dissolving of the military dictatorship came Islamic extremism. Alhadji Ahmed Sani, governor of the Nigerian northern state of Zamfara, began the political transformation on 27 October 1999, when he proclaimed that his state would henceforth be governed by Sharia law. Sani modeled his legal system on that of Saudi Arabia, a country he admired very much. The effect of this declaration caused eleven other states in northern Nigeria to implement Sharia law (McCormack 2005, 11). The introduction of democracy into Nigeria, which allowed for the election of a Christian president, had a combined effect of alienating the Muslims in the north and opening the door for them to look to outside Islamic governments for support.

The resurgence of Islamic fundamentalism in Nigeria in 1999 was influenced by an infusion of Saudi-educated religious scholars who challenged less austere versions of Islam. Islamic fundamentalism acquired a more pronounced political edge as the national fortunes of the governing Muslim national elite declined dramatically with the election of President Obasanjo, a born-again Christian from the south. After playing a major, often dominant role in the government and military for almost forty years, northern Muslims felt sidelined. Among the reasons for these feelings was Obasanjo's removal of politicized military officers, who were disproportionately Muslim (Dickson 2005).

The historical ties Islam has to northern Nigeria have been reinforced generation by generation through an Islamic education system. The term "Madrassas" has been used in recent years as a generic term to refer to an Islamic education system. Nigeria, like other Muslim-dominated countries, has a long history of Islamic education. In the early stages of its introduction into West Africa, Islam in general influenced education and encouraged debates and experimentation. Historically Islam in Africa and specifically Nigeria was not very extreme. However, with the introduction of Sunni Islam

Wahhabism, the education system became increasingly extreme, characterized by simply memorizing the Koran and Hadith (Awofeso et al. 2003, 312).

Religious schools funded by Saudi Arabia teach Wahhabism, which amounts to preaching Wahhabism. The Aljamiri heritage is, like the Madrassas in Central Asia, a system of Muslim education that dates back several centuries. The Almajiri Heritage system contains four important features that make it ideal for exploitation by an extremist movement. First, it involves children being relocated--separated from their village family and friends to the guardianship of Mallams in towns. Second, it is restricted almost exclusively to boys. Third, the curriculum of the schools is concerned primarily with teaching the sixty chapters of the Koran by rote memorization. Fourth, each school serves 25 to 500 students, from the ages six to twenty-five. These schools are largely autonomous from government oversight (Awofeso et al. 2003, 314).

Muslim youth of northern Nigeria are being indoctrinated into an extreme Islamic ideology. This indoctrinated youth will be exploited by the global Islamic extremist insurgency to further the Islamic extremist cause. In fact, according to Mustafa Setmarian Nasar, who is a senior Al Qaeda ideologue, the most effective method to foster the emergence of new local Jihadi movements is to keep Muslim clerics actively involved at the local level to train, educate, and indoctrinate the next generation of Jihadis, who will eventually sweep away the old order. These Madrassas are a key aspect of this program (Brachman and McCants 2006, 15, 17).

Ideology binds modern Islamic extremism in Africa to what the US knows as the Al Qaeda Associated Movement. The existence of Al Qaeda-affiliated or franchised Islamic extremist groups operating in North Africa is an important indicator that Nigeria

34

is operating as a safe haven for the global Islamic extremist movement. After the 1998 embassy bombings in Kenya and Tanzania, the US government suspended diplomatic and business operations in countries that, in 1998, were known to have an Al Qaeda presence: Somalia, Sudan, Congo, and Guinea-Bissau. Many in the intelligence community who were following Osama bin Laden felt the Islamic extremists were trying to expand from the traditional Islamic areas of Northern Africa to Central and West Africa. Plans were set in motion for further attacks against US embassies as a means of politicizing and radicalizing African Muslims, in hopes of provoking anti-Muslim backlashes in the countries concerned (Gunaratna 2002, 217).

In 1998 Al Qaeda had unfettered freedom of movement to West and Central Africa. The Al Qaeda Islamic extremist movement organizational structure depends on clusters or families who are regionally and ethnically related to run organizations. As a general rule Tunisians work within Tunisian cells, Egyptians work within Egyptian cells, and so forth. Al Qaeda has a global reach because of its ability to appeal to Muslims irrespective of their nationality, giving it unprecedented resources. It can function in East Asia, in Russia, in the heart of Europe, in Sub-Saharan Africa, and throughout Canada and the US with equal facility. Islamic extremists have overcome cultural and linguistic barriers in an innovative fashion: they organized their families regionally and functionally (Gunaratna 2002, 129-130).

The Group for Preaching Combat (GSPC) provides the regional nexus between the Islamic extremist leadership in Nigeria, and the global Islamic extremist movement. In West Africa, Al Qaeda has leveraged existing Islamic extremist organizations, along with an infrastructure established in corrupt countries, to further its ideological aims. One example of how Islamic extremists operated in West Africa is illustrated by the relationship they built with Charles Taylor, the former brutal dictator of Liberia, who is now in living in Nigeria.

> On July 25, Ahmed Khalfan Ghailani was arrested in eastern Pakistan along with more than a dozen other Qaeda operatives and is being held in connection with the 1998 bombings of two U.S. embassies in Africa. For at least three years, beginning in the late 1990s, however, he lived in an army camp and hotels run by Taylor's government in Liberia. In addition, according to US officials and UN investigators, Taylor's forces harbored other suspected Al Qaeda leaders, including MIT-educated biologist Aafia Siddiqui. Al Qaeda allegedly paid Taylor for protection and then joined him in the African diamond trade, raising millions of dollars for terrorist activities, according to U.N. war crimes documents. It is clear that Al Qaeda had been in West Africa since September 1998 and maintained a continuous presence in the area through 2002, according to a new confidential report by the UN Special Court for Sierra Leone. (Bender 2004)

Amazingly enough, in view of the 9/11 Commission's denial of Nigeria as a safe haven, open-source reporting had earlier established a conscious effort by Islamic extremists to establish a base of operation in West Africa, particularly in Nigeria. In a message delivered by the leader of Al Qaeda in February 2003, two years before the 11 September Report denied the existence of Islamic extremist in Nigeria, Osama bin Laden identified Nigeria as one of five apostate states ripe for revolution, confirming the desire of the global Islamic extremist movement to expand into Nigeria (McCormack 2005, 11). Furthermore, the activities of the Algerian terrorist group, the Salafist GSPC, in the Sahel countries of West Africa, from Mauritania to Niger Republic, including Nigeria, are stated sources of concern to Nigerian law enforcement. Open-source reporting has established the fact that there were three Nigerians who were among the GSPC combatants captured (several more were killed) by Chadian soldiers during an exchange of fire between Chadian forces and GSPC terrorists in April 2004. Moreover, "[i]n July 2005, operatives of the Nigerian Intelligence Agency interrogated one Al-Qaeda

36

operative in Tripoli, Libya, who confirmed that he was sent to Nigeria by Al-Qaeda in late 2003 to arrange a number of targets for it. He successfully concluded his assignment and sent his reports to his handlers in Afghanistan through a Nigerian he recruited before leaving the country in October 2004. The Nigerian was arrested by Pakistani authorities while trying to return to Nigeria, having delivered the Al-Qaeda operatives work to their handlers" (Foreign Broadcast Information Service 2005). This would indicate there is a mechanism for GSPC recruitment, training, and placement in Nigeria.

With the history of Islam in Nigeria, the Saudi Arabian funding backing Wahhabist schools, and the reports of Islamic extremist franchised movements, Nigeria has proven to be an ideal target for Islamic extremist ideology. This is the first indicator that Nigeria is a safe haven for Islamic extremists.

The second indicator that Nigeria is a safe haven for Islamic extremists is that the resources to support a safe haven exist within Nigeria. Resources in relation to Islamic extremist networks have been defined as "a person, organization, place, or thing (physical or non-physical) and its attributes" (Joint Chiefs of Staff 2006, 14). The following resources exist in Nigeria that would help to support a safe haven: organized crime, Saudi Arabian funding, and traditional trading routes.

Islamic extremists are able to transfer people and equipment, raise and launder money, and spread their message through a link-up to the unfettered, unregulated World Wide Web, all through organized crime. Corruption and organized crime are exploited by regional Islamic extremists to connect to the global organized criminal network (Farah 2003, 49). Nigerian criminal groups have provided important documents, to include false passports and fake credit cards, to Al Qaeda for entry into France, Italy, and Great

Britain. Islamic extremists are also alleged to have exploited the underground West African diamond trade to hide assets to the tune of 240 million US dollars, which the US Central Intelligence Agency believes has been used to purchase a wide array of weaponry, including assault rifles, rocket-propelled grenades, and surface-to-air missiles (Rabasa et al. 2004, 428).

The US Department of State now specifically recognizes the sophisticated Nigerian organized crime groups as one of the single most important elements driving the international trafficking of heroin and cocaine, especially to the North American market. Nigerian organized criminals rival the Russians and Chinese as the most capable in the world. According to its 2002 International Narcotics Control Strategy Report, Nigeria is a central hub of narcotics trafficking and money laundering. Organized crime groups in the country dominate the African drug trade. Nigerians are known masterminds at complex drug trafficking. They are specialists at moving narcotics and choosing many different routes to the US successfully (Chalk 2003, 4). Organized crime syndicates have established practices allowing them to smuggle drugs throughout the world. This is a global problem; however, if the money raised through this drug trade is invested back into the global Islamic extremist insurgency, it makes it difficult to shut off financial resources to the Islamic extremists. More worrisome, however, would be if Islamic extremists use the same smuggling routes and techniques to move weapons of mass destruction to the US. Organized crime in Nigeria is a valuable resource when it comes to supporting the Islamic extremist's ideology.

Besides using the resource of organized crime to facilitate Islamic extremist operations, the Saudi Arabian government has been linked to nongovernmental organizations (NGOs) and charities that raise money for the Islamic extremist movement. Al-Muntada, an agency headed by Dr. Adil ibn Muhammad al-Saleem and based in Great Britain, is associated with the official Saudi state charitable and da'wa institutions, the Muslim World League, World Assembly of Muslim Youth (WAMY), International Islamic Relief Organization, and al-Haramain Islamic Foundation, all alleged by American and international investigators to be terror-financing bodies. Dr. Adil ibn Muhammad al-Saleem's NGOs have been particularly active in promoting Wahhabi-style Islam in Nigeria. Al-Muntada pays for Nigerian clerics to be trained in Saudi universities and then returned to Nigeria through a well-funded network of mosques and schools to promote Wahhabi-style Islamic extremism (Marshal 2004).

Saudi Arabian funding through charities in poor regions of Nigeria provides legitimacy and access for Islamic extremists. These "charities," which are directly controlled by Saudi Arabian government officials, bring medication and badly needed supplies to targeted populations in Nigeria. This access and funding set the conditions for Islamic extremists to recruit, build infrastructure, spread their message, and gain the tacit support of the populations.

In testimony before the US Senate Committee on the Judiciary Terrorism, Two Years After 9/11, Connecting the Dots, Simon Henderson, a Saudi strategies expert, gives a very detailed description of Saudi Arabian Wahhabist roles in funding and globally exporting their brand of Islam. The testimony establishes linkages between Saudi-funded Wahhabist charities and the global Islamic extremist insurgency. Examining how the Saudi-funded WAMY operates is instructive and can be applied to most Saudi Arabian charity organizations. According to WAMY's British website its purpose is "to serve the true Islamic ideology based on Tawheed, the Unity of God," (Tawheed is a reference to the Wahhabi form of Islam), and to coordinate Islamic youth organizations across the world. WAMY represents fifty-five countries, associates membership with over 500 youth organizations around the world, and is recognized by the United Nations as an NGO for its humanitarian and relief work in the Muslim world. It is responsible for building mosques and Islamic centers around the globe (Henderson 2003).

Steve Emerson, a US expert on global terrorism, details how WAMY is linked to the global Islamic extremist insurgency. WAMY's education is not limited to Islamic theology. When the Al-Qaeda-affiliated terrorist Ahmed Ajaj was arrested and convicted in connection with the 1993 World Trade Center bombing, investigators confiscated his belongings. Among them was an official WAMY envelope printed with the organization's return address in Saudi Arabia. The envelope contained a manual titled "Military Lessons in the *Jihad* Against the Tyrants," detailing how to establish and maintain clandestine cells. Another version of the same manual, with several added sections, was found in the London apartment of African Embassy bomber Khalid al-Fawwaz in 1998. Fawwaz has since been indicted, and the US is seeking his extradition from England.

The Ajaj manual refers repeatedly to the role and importance of youth in carrying out Jihad and re-establishing Muslim rule. The manual's dedication says, "what [the apostate regimes] know is the dialogue of bullets, the ideals of assassination, explosion and destruction, and the politics of the machine gun." It continues:

> An Islamic state has not and will not be formed through peaceful solutions or through the Assemblies of Polytheism. It will be formed as it did through the written words and the gun, through the word and the bullet.' The manual instructs

'the principal mission for the military organization is to overthrow the atheist regimes and replace them with Islamic ones,' and lists strategies such as kidnapping enemy soldiers, assassinating personnel and foreign tourists, spreading rumors, and blowing up, destroying, and sabotaging places of entertainment as secondary duties of the military organization. The ultimate goal, repeated over and over, is get[ting] rid of people who stand in the way of the Islamic Call, and establishing an Islamic State. (Emerson 2003)

The established track record of Saudi Arabian charities and their association with Islamic extremism is compelling. The following is a press release from the Saudi Arabian Information Bureau:

In November of 2003 WAMY organized one hundred Nigerian secondary school students participated in a 15-day educational youth camp organized by the Riyadh-based World Assembly of Muslim Youth (WAMY), which featured a variety of programs, workshops, video shows and symposiums. Dr Abdulwahab Noorwali, WAMY's Assistant Secretary General, said that the camp was held in the Nigerian town of Borno, with the aim of raising awareness among youth and developing their skills to serve their communities. He pointed out that the camp is the third of its kind to be organized for secondary school students in Nigeria. WAMY is making in roads into Nigeria. (Saudi Arabian Information Resource 2006)

"Islamic extremists have infiltrated NGOs operating in Sub Saharan Africa. According to western intelligence sources, 90 percent of the international Islamic NGOs operating in Uganda were either established or operated by Arabs with funding from the Middle East" (Gunaratna 2002, 218). Islamic extremists have coordinated operations with Saudi-Arabian-funded charity organizations that operate globally. The regional capability resident in NGOs, along with the quasi-diplomatic status some of the NGOs maintain through the United Nations, means that Islamic extremists are positioned to coordinate operations in West Africa, in some instances more effectively and with a more regional emphasis than the US State Department USAID. "The Saudi Foreign Ministry and its network of embassies provide a crucial structure for propagating Wahhabism and distributing state funds to support the growth of Wahhabism across the world"

41

(Henderson 2003). All organizations need financial resources to exist and to achieve their goals. Nigeria's population of Islamic extremists is being funded, in part, by Saudi Arabia in order to meet theirs.

Another resource of Nigeria is its trade routes, which are controlled by local Islamic leaders. Islam in northern Nigeria is connected to what is referred to as the "dirt belt." This geographical area runs west from Sudan across Chad, Cameroon, and northern Nigeria, and historically has been a trading belt that has been run locally by African Islamic emirs, the local Muslim leaders. The emirs in northern Nigeria have a degree of autonomy from the central government. This author's own experience in northern Cameroon, a country that borders Nigeria, confirms this. This author witnessed firsthand how the local Lamido (Emir) acts as the religious figurehead for Islam in the village or town and performs many other functions, the most important of which are bank manager and judge ruling over local disputes, as well as a "godfather" who helps solve disputes between people who are outside the "normal" judiciary power. This form of local government, which is similar to the local government in northern Nigeria, if left alone and immune from outside influence, is an effective way of governing through established local customs and practices. When the local emir is manipulated through outside influence by Islamic extremist ideology, however, it is an effective vehicle to impose an extremist ideology and control a region at the grassroots level. Because the location of these emirs is along the dirt belt, they can be used effectively and efficiently to move people, money, and ideology from the horn of Africa to Mali, thus making Nigeria's trade routes a very valuable resource for Islamic extremists.

Poor government control is the third and final indicator that Nigeria is a safe haven for Islamic extremists. Nigeria is made up of a federal government that exercises weak control over thirty-six states. Another example of the weak central government control is that in the last seven years northern Nigeria has officially established a Sharia law judicial system in twelve of the thirty-six states. Nigeria sits along tribal, religious, economic, political, and judicial and legal fault lines. Add to this potent mixture an externally financed ideology, targeted rhetoric of Islamic extremism, a substantial organized criminal network, and wealth disparity, and the potential for Islamic extremists to establish a network capable of supporting global ambitions is real.

Nigeria is almost equally divided between Christians and Muslims. The lack of a strong central government, little or no distribution of the Nigerian oil wealth, corruption, and organized crime make Nigeria an exploitable entity for Islamic extremists. The twelve states in northern Nigeria, which operate under their own judicial system, have been and currently are the scene of deadly clashes between Christians and Muslims. At the local level fighting takes on an ethnic or religious character; since Christianity and the Yoruba and Ibo people are associated with the south, and Islam and the Hausa people with the north, the country is divided almost equally along religious lines. Usually the conflict has been sparked by local rivalries, but fueled by wider regional resentments, whether commercially or politically based. Out of Nigeria's total thirty-six states, all twelve northern states have embraced Sharia law, which has caused 7,000 to 10,000 deaths in clashes stimulated by religious conflict since 1999 (Botha and Solomon 2002, 10). The global "cartoon" riots in January and February of 2006, arising from the depiction of Mohammed in an editorial cartoon in a Danish newspaper, have killed more than 140 people in the country, as of the writing of this thesis, and the death toll continues to rise. On 9 February 2006, the Information Minister for Nigeria, Frank Nweke, accused the Kano state of seeking foreign assistance to train one hundred Jihadists in the areas of intelligence and the practice of Jihad (Ahemba 2006). This division causes instability within the government, creating lack of control over its people.

Natural resources in Nigeria also contribute to religious division in the country. The oil in Nigeria is located in the southern portion of the country, which is dominated by Christians. Wealth distribution from the profits from oil is almost nonexistent. A World Bank report released in October 2004 indicated that up to 80 percent of revenues from Nigeria's oil industry accrue to only one percent of the general population. In January 2005, two Nigerian Navy admirals were convicted of facilitating the theft of an oil tanker in August 2004, confirming long-held suspicions of theft of crude oil for profit, with Navy officers often colluding with criminals. In the same month, Nigeria's Economic and Financial Crimes Commission began to investigate allegations of tax evasion by multinational oil companies in collusion with government officials. In February 2005, the Nigerian government began an investigation into the illegal existence of 193 unlicensed airstrips and helipads operated by large multinational oil companies (eia.doe.gov 2006). The lack of wealth distribution and endemic corruption is leveraged by the foreign Islamic extremists in Nigeria to rally northern Muslims against Christians in the southern Nigeria.

The fact is that that twelve states within Nigeria practice Sharia law. This form of Islamic governance is a powerful tool to maintain control and establish authority over a region. Sharia law is not practiced in the country as a whole and it is an Islamic form of

44

government. Nigeria lives under two distinctively different judicial systems. In effect, the implementation of Sharia law has created a state within a state. This dichotomy in the national judicial systems fuels disparities in Nigeria between Christians living in northern Nigeria and Muslims.

The implementation of Sharia law in northern Nigeria should not be brushed aside. The state-enforced imposition of Sharia law is central to the projection of Islamist extremism worldwide, whether in Iraq, Nigeria, Tajikistan, or Indonesia. The explicit, continually reiterated program is, in brief, to restore a politically unified worldwide Muslim community, the "ummah," ruled by a single ruler, a "caliph," governed by the most reactionary version of Islamic law, "Sharia," and organized to wage "Jihad" on the rest of the world (Glazov 2005).

The use of the Internet as a resource for Islamic extremists in Nigeria is facilitated by the lack of control the central government has in regulating its exploitation by Islamic extremists. Nigeria's Internet service providers and cyber cafés operate in a highly deregulated telecommunications industry. The Internet arrived there impromptu and, in most cases, it bypasses local infrastructure. Most Nigerian Internet traffic is nonlocal; rather, it gets routed to a very small aperture terminal, which is a small-sized telecommunications earth station that transmits and receives via satellite. The terminal size is 1.2 to 2.4 meters in diameter. Very small aperture terminals are becoming increasingly popular, because they are a single, flexible communications platform that can be installed quickly and cost effectively in remote regions of the world. It is a highly decentralized operating environment, mostly outside the control of government (Oysanya 2004).

45

The capture of an Al Qaeda operative, Muhammad Naeem Noor Khan, provided the Pakistani and American intelligence authorities with some of Al Qaeda's Internet communications strategy. It also identified that Nigerian websites and email systems were used by Al Qaeda to disseminate Internet information. Terrorist information flow used Nigeria as its gateway. The choice of using Nigerian email systems and websites shows how careful and thorough Al Qaeda's computer operatives are. It is not an act of coincidence, but a case of choosing the perfect environment for passing undetected terrorist Internet information. Nigerian Internet space provides a virtual "cyber cave" in which Islamic extremist can hide. Nigeria's information technology infrastructure offers terrorists one of the best paths for transmitting email and web-based information, largely because most of Nigeria's Internet system does not provide the minimum level of information assurance.

The central government's ability to control its cyber environment is nonexistent. Nigeria is the home of Internet scams and credit card theft because the government has no ability to stop it. Like other aspects of Nigeria that make it an attractive place for an Islamic extremist, the cyber world is no exception. The core groups of Al Qaeda Islamic extremists are reported to be computer knowledgeable. Their ability to leverage the Internet and mass media to project their ideology, conduct training, and, to some extent, command and control operations is amplified by the global information grid. As one report states, "Nigeria is a place where you can use the computer to commit various forms of Internet crime and evade prosecution, because there is no national legal jurisdiction on cyber crime. If there was ever a crime such as Internet murder Nigeria would be the place to commit it" (Oysanya 2004).

Poor government control allows for freedom of movement, whether one is moving information freely via the Internet or physically moving diamonds, for example. Analyzing the Islamic extremists' premeditated move to establish control over the diamond trade in West Africa offers insight into the freedom of movement and the previously existing infrastructure in West Africa for Islamic extremists. The very detailed account offered by Douglas Farah, in which he retraces the Islamic extremist movement to secure and corner the diamond market in West Africa in the late 1990s, should be instructive to US government officials. Farah states that regionally there has been cooperation between the Al Qaeda Islamic extremists and the Hezballah Shi'a Islamic extremists. There is virtually no capability existent in the individual governments in the region capable of denying Islamic extremists the use of West Africa, including Nigeria, to further their cause. Through detailed investigative reporting he states that Abdullah Ahmed Abdullah (described by the FBI as a top bin Laden adviser), Khalfan Ghailani, and Fazul Abdullah Mohammad, all associated with al-Qaeda and wanted by the FBI in connection with the Tanzanian and Kenya bombing, were in Liberia buying diamonds (Farah 2003, 56).

CHAPTER 4

CONCLUSIONS AND RECOMMENDATIONS

Conclusions

As stated in the introduction of this paper, the CRS produced a report on Safe Havens and Sanctuaries, which not only did not identify Nigeria as a country requiring "immediate concern" as a sanctuary or a safe haven, but also declared that Nigeria becoming such a safe haven was highly unlikely: "While Nigeria could potentially provide sanctuary for terrorists, at present such an outcome appears to be only a theoretical possibility" (Miko 2004, 20).

A review of news sources and informal discussions with US officials indicates that there appear to be few "overt" or apparent indications that there is a current or immediate threat of an international presence in the Mano River Basin countries; Sierra Leone, Liberia, and Guinea, in addition to Nigeria. While Nigeria has a large Muslim population that includes some radical elements and supporters of Salafist-oriented theologies, as well as numerous self-professed admirers of Osama bin Laden, religious-linked threats to Nigerian national security have primarily taken the form of recurrent Muslim-Christian violence in central and northern Nigeria and in the commercial capital, Lagos (Miko 2004, 20-22).

This research in contrast to the 9-11 CRS Report does, however, identify the existence of Islamic extremist safe havens in Nigeria. The indicators are divided into three broad categories: existence of Islamic extremist ideology, existence of resources and indicators supporting the ideological goals of Islamic extremism, and a description of the central government in Nigeria revealing a lack of capability to counter Islamic

48

extremist ideology or the ability to curtail resources available to the Islamic extremist operations.

The Islamic extremists' stated vision, as defined earlier in the research, and here using the words of Islamic extremist themselves, is the creation of a "Caliphate" running from Western Europe to Central Asia. Part of this vision requires the indoctrination of the next generation of young Muslims into an extreme form of Islam. This extreme Islamic ideology in historical context was explained earlier in the paper.

The global Islamic extremists are waging a generational war. They target resources to indoctrinate the next generation of "Jihadist" through structured religious schooling, empowering local clerics to mold the youth into the next generation of Islamic extremists. In Nigeria, this manifests itself in the form of "Madrassas." Nigeria has hundreds of well-funded Madrassas, insuring the promulgation of the Islamic extremist ideology into Nigerian society.

As previously explained, the global Islamic extremist insurgency is well adapted at utilizing NGOs and charity organizations and setting conditions at the local and regional levels for exploitation. Nigeria has several of these "Islamic charities" operating in country. They are able to provide some basic needs to a population that might not otherwise receive them from a weak local, state, or federal government, thus gaining acceptance. Charities like WAMY, as highlighted in this paper, actively train and recruit future members to Islamic extremism, creating conditions favorable to spreading their ideology.

This research paper asks: Are there endemic characteristics and resources in Nigeria making it a place where Islamic extremists can be successful? The research defined resources as the existence of those functions required by the Islamic extremist to promulgate their ideology and to plan and project operations. Nigeria specifically, and West Africa in general remain crippled by rampant corruption and organized crime. Nigeria's organized criminal infrastructure reaches into Pakistan and Afghanistan and is ready made for global exploitation by the Islamic extremist insurgency. The research highlights money laundering, document forgery and diamond smuggling as functions present in Nigeria supporting current and future Islamic extremist operations.

As reported and documented from various sources, the consensus describes the central government of Nigeria as lacking the capability to control the porous borders, stop corruption, manage the religious division among Christians and Muslims, curtail organized crime, and fairly distribute the vast oil wealth. In a country of 124 million people the impotence of the central government by default allows Islamic extremists to promote their ideology, plan operations, and recruit potential members. Taken together, these realities all contribute to the establishment of an Islamic extremist operational global infrastructure, creating an environment in which Islamic extremism can thrive.

The location of the natural resources in Nigeria's Christian south and the lack of wealth distribution contribute further to the growing animosity between Christians and Muslims; as a result there have been several thousand Nigerians killed in religious strife since 1999.

The existence of Sharia law in twelve of the northern states of Nigeria further illustrates the central government's lack of capability to project its influence throughout the country. This weakness of government leadership and control suggests Islamic extremists will capitalize further to extend and entrench themselves in the region.

Islamic extremist are continuing to promote internal strife in Nigeria between Muslims and Christians. A robust Islamic extremist recruitment is fueled by Nigerian Muslims being killed by Nigerian Christians and cleverly reported via Global Internet communications. This continuing Muslim-Christian conflict in Nigeria has a destabilizing effect on relatively stable African countries like Senegal, Mali, Cameroon, and Uganda. At the time of this writing, the recent cartoon riots have caused the death of approximately 145 Christian and Muslim Nigerians. The potential to foment internal strife within Nigeria and threaten the US oil supply must be an appealing thought to Islamic extremist leaders and planners.

The research points to the fact that where Islam is supported by Saudi Arabian Wahabism, established organized crime exists, and a corrupt and or weak central government is in charge, Islamic extremists will be operating within that region. The global Islamic extremist insurgency must have a logistical basis in order to project power. Predictably insurgents will seek regions or countries offering freedom of movement both physically and virtually. Insurgents need a financial infrastructure, immune from Western monitoring that can sustain regional and global operations. They need knowledgeable "Jihadists" with English-language skills that allow them to operate in Western countries.

In the short term, there is very little the US can do to affect what this author sees as the current establishment of Islamic extremist safe havens in Nigeria and West Africa. Programs like the PSI are excellent starts, but they lack an essential urgency and focus, along with a coordinated interagency approach necessary to be most effective in West Africa and Nigeria. The global Islamic extremists in Nigeria effectively leverage localized links with organized crime and cyber access. The Islamic extremists now exist in safe havens conveniently available in northern Nigeria, furthering their violent cause. Clearly, Nigeria is a foothold for Islamic extremists to extend their influence into West Africa. If this threat is left unchallenged the global Islamic presence in Nigeria will be used to destabilize other countries in Africa and easily facilitate potential attacks against the West.

The paper exposes the fact that the US government's conceptual idea of a safe haven has not kept up with the Islamic extremists' capability to use twenty-first century technology. As a result the US government does not properly categorize or identify the function of a safe haven. Regions, both physical and nonphysical, that is, virtual, via the global information grid, provide functions that insurgents use to promote their ideological manipulations of information and to assist in projecting power. The twentieth-century notion of a safe haven as only a physical location on the ground in which insurgents rest, plan, and launch attacks simply does not apply to today's dangerous Islamic extremist operations. Islamic extremists cleverly leverage the global information grid to plan, command and control, train, recruit, spread their ideology, and attack US interests from almost all reaches of the globe. Islamic extremists can easily raise money to attack US interests using charities and NGOs located inside the US. They have active planning cells inside countries the US considers friends or allies. Islamic extremists also leverage organized criminal networks raising money and transporting personnel around the globe.

The research asserts that Nigeria is operating as an Islamic extremist safe haven. In February 2003, even the leader of the global Islamic extremist insurgency, Osama bin Laden, called Nigeria one of the most qualified regions for religious and political liberations. Yet, exactly two years later, the CRS Report, *Removing Terrorist*

Sanctuaries: The 9/11 Commission Recommendations and U.S Policy, failed to identify Nigeria as a terrorist safe haven. This measured amateur characterization of Nigeria by the CRS directly impacts US legislative policy, wasting valuable planning and preparation time the US government needs to establish a strategy for managing the global Islamic insurgency in West Africa. The 11 September Report on Removing Terrorist Sanctuaries illustrates how poorly the author of the report understands the global nature of the Islamic extremist insurgency and the nature and requirements of the insurgency sanctuary. The wording in this report that is most troubling states that there is no immediate threat of an international terrorist presence in Nigeria (Miko 2004, 22). Unfortunately when Nigeria is recognized as an immediate threat to the US it will be too late to generate sufficient national power to prevent or to fix the problem. The goal of US policy ought to be to proactively identify countries and regions before they become safe havens and sanctuaries for the global Islamic extremist insurgency movement.

Nigeria is a regional power and strategically important to the US; located near vast oil and natural gas reserves, it is linked to critical regions in West Africa, pointing north to Europe and west towards the US. This research argues that Nigeria is an Islamic extremist safe haven, making Nigeria an important country for US national security reasons. The research describes the modern history and evolution and dangers of Islamic ideology, particularly within Nigeria's Muslim communities. Also reviewed here were the availability of resources, technology, and funding that support Islamic extremism in Nigeria. Finally, the paper expresses concern about the lack of knowledge, preparation and proactive efforts from US policy makers to adequately define and address the Islamic extremist threat. This deficiency allows for further expansion of the Islamic extremist threat to the US and the world.

Recommendations

The research indicates the US is at war with an Islamic extremist insurgency that uses terrorism as one of many tactics to attack the US and its allies. US government policy should not define the enemy only as a "terrorist," but rather focus on revealing the true nature and goals of Islamic extremism, its characteristics and symptoms, providing clear policy guidance describing exact indicators of the global Islamic extremist operations.

The US government should identify and characterize clear indicators of Islamic extremism, thus enabling individual embassies, under the Secretary of State and in close coordination with Department of Defense, to act quickly to counter the enemy, utilizing the full breadth of the US national power. As much as the US has created a myth that the enemy is decentralized, this research consistently found common ideological and strategic threads running through all Islamic extremist organizations with which the US is now at war. It is imperative to clearly articulate these important indicators of Islamic extremism in order to focus the US government's information operations capabilities against the enemy. The US government must articulate the true nature and goals of the global Islamic extremist insurgency in order to help the American people to understand the dangerous intent of the Islamic extremist.

The Wahhabist ideological message should not go unchallenged. This is the foundation for many Islamic extremists that enables them to mobilize a mass following. It is baffling how an exclusionary sect of Islam can go unchallenged by other Islamic sects and by other moderate religions and concerned governments.

It is necessary to recognize that Islam in West Africa generally is not extreme, and when it is extreme it is not dangerous until well funded and clearly manipulated by global Islamic extremists. The US must now actively counter this extremist ideological message. This can be done by investing resources in countries like Senegal and Mali, where Islam is a religion and not yet a form of government. These countries should and can be a model for Africa, demonstrating to the world how to fairly incorporate Islam within a secular government. The US should commit necessary and sufficient instruments of national power to insure that Senegal and Mali are connected to the positive aspects of globalization.

The US government should create environments inhospitable to the Islamic extremist message. Without a unifying message or agitator, sixty-eight million Muslims in Nigeria remain a Nigerian problem. With a unifying message and an agitator, Nigeria's sixty-eight million Muslims become a regional and international problem. A major challenge facing US policy makers is how to formulate an information operation campaign that will attack the ideological foundation of the Islamic extremism. In order to win the "long war" US policy makers should examine what information operation would "blunt" the current ideology the Islamic extremist use to influence the Ummah. Winning the ideological battle of the next generation in the Ummah is critical for winning the long war against terrorism.

Within Nigeria the US State Department must counter the Wahhabist message in northern Nigeria. PSI is a positive beginning. This type of initiative must be coordinated throughout West Africa through a lead federal agency and all instruments of national power used to check Islamic extremism. Programs like PSI could represent positive direction for US policy in this region of the world. PSI offers a template for how the US can most effectively combat growing Islamic extremism in vulnerable regions of Africa, such as Nigeria. These programs recognize the requirement to integrate both Department of State and Department of Defense strategies to better fight Islamic extremism.

During the Cold War the US intelligence community studied the ideologies of Karl Marx and Frederick Engels in order to understand the Soviet Union. General Abizaid, Commander US Central Command, said in testimony to the House Armed Services Committee in September 2004 that the Islamic extremist "will try to re-establish a caliphate throughout the entire Muslim world," adding that the caliphate's goals would include the destruction of Israel. "Just as we had the opportunity to learn what the Nazis were going to do, from Hitler's world in 'Mein Kampf,' we need to learn what these people intend to do from their own words" (Bumiller 2004, 2). The enemy has published and continues to publish his strategic message and operational intent. General Abizaid's guidance about understanding the Islamic extremist strategic goals and intent by studying open-source documents produced by the Islamic extremists themselves should take a higher priority in US academia and by US government policy makers. It is imperative that the US government policy makers and the US citizens grasp the magnitude of the Islamic extremist threat and its growing influence in vulnerable regions of the world.

Topics for Further Research

The author's overall recommendation for further research would be topics that lead to a better understanding of Islam. In conducting research on the subject of Islamic extremism in Nigeria, the author encountered questions which require further research to better educate US policy makers about the nature of the enemy against whom the US is currently at war. If the author had unlimited time and resources the following broad categories would receive attention: apply the author's model to past insurgencies; identify the characteristics of moderate Islam, the long-term social impact Wahhabism, and US strategic interest in West Africa.

The author has proposed three simple indicators that can be used to identify an Islamic extremist safe haven in Nigeria. The author recommends a topic for further research focusing on past insurgencies and comparing and contrasting the similarities between what those insurgencies require of a safe haven and what the global Islamic extremists require. Are the indicators the author proposed unique to "networked" global Islamic extremism? Have the global Islamic extremists adapted to modern information age technology so dramatically that their organization changed the nature a safe haven? Research on these topics would further educate US policy makers and academia on the nature of the enemy we are currently at war.

Almost five years after the 11 September attack, US policy makers have yet to fully appreciate the depth and the scope of Islamic extremism. When the author adds words behind "Islamic" like "extremist," "radical," or "terrorist," by default there is an implication that there is a separate Islam from the extremist radical Islam. A topic for further research would be indicators of moderate Islam. If there exists a moderate voice of Islam, who or what organization is representing this view? If there is a moderate voice in the Muslim Ummah, how can the US work with it to defeat the extremist or radical Islamic ideology? Who individually and what institutions represent moderate Islam? How does one identify moderate Islam within the Ummah, and determine what influence the moderate voices of Islam have on the entirety of the Ummah?

Another topic one could further research is focusing on the impact the Wahhabi Madrassas have had on the millions of youth "educated" since the early 1970s; of the tens of million Muslim youth educated in these Madrassas and the billions of dollars spent on Wahhabist causes since the early 1970s, what has been the result? How many doctors, engineers, teachers, farmers, bankers, lawyers have been produced through this education system? What is the impact on the societies when those who have been educated in the Madrassas return to live among them? What has been the impact of "brainwashing" students to hate Jews, Christians, and all things not Islam? Huntington argues that Muslims are at war with their Catholic, Protestant, Orthodox, Hindu, Chinese, Buddhist, and Jewish neighbors at a higher rate then between groups from other civilizations (1996, 256). Can this claim be correlated to the Saudi Arabian Wahhabist money spent during the last thirty years?

A topic for further research would be what the US long-term goal in West Africa is, and what its strategic understanding of West Africa is in relation to Islamic extremism's Caliphate aspirations? "Imports of African oil are projected to grow from their current 15 percent of the US total to 25 percent by 2015. The US already imports more oil from Africa than Saudi Arabia, and within a decade it could become a greater source of oil imports than the whole of the Persian Gulf" (Booker and Colgan 2006). Africa has strategic importance to the US, which will only grow as its dependence on oil from this region increases. Has US policy and understanding of Africa kept pace with the strategic importance of the continent?

REFERENCE LIST

Ahemba, Tume. 2006. Reuters AlertNet: Nigeria state seeks foreign aid for jihadists-gov't. Available from http://www.alertnet.org/thenews/newsdesl/L09557323.htm. Internet. Accessed on 9 February 2006.

Armstrong, Karen. 2000. *The battle for god: A history of fundamentalism.* New York, NY: The Ballantine Publishing Group.

Awofeso, Niyi, J. E. Ritchie, and P. J. Degeling. 2003. The Almajiri heritage and the threat of non-state terrorism in northern Nigeria--Lessons from Central Asia and Pakistan. *Studies in Conflict and Terrorism* 26, no. 4 (July-August): 311-325.

Back, Irit. 2002. *Osama bin Laden's African progress.* Tel Aviv Notes, no. 58 (December). Article on-line. Available from http://www.tau.ac.il/jcss/ tanotes/TAUnotes58.doc. Internet. Accessed on 10 October 2005.

Baran, Zeyno. 2005. Combating al-Qaeda and the militant Islamic threat. Testimony before US House of Representatives Committee Armed Services, Subcommittee on Terrorism, Unconventional Threats and Capabilities. Available from http://counterterror.typepad.com/the_counterterrorism_blog/files/ barancongress_testimony_feb_06.DOC. Internet. Accessed on 18 April 2006.

Bender, Bryan, Globe Staff. 2004. Liberia's Taylor gave aid to Qaeda, UN probe finds. Article on-line. Available from http://www.boston.com/news/world/articles/2004/ 08/04/liberias_taylor_gave_aid_to_qaeda_un_probe_finds/. Internet. Accessed on 8 March 2006.

Berry, Laverle, Glenn E. Curtis, John N. Gibbs, Rex A. Hudson, Tara Karacan, Nina Kollars, and Ramon Miro. 2003. *Nations hospitable to organized crime and terrorism.* Washington, DC: Federal Research Division, Library of Congress. Available from http://www.loc.gov/rr/frd/pdf-files/Nats_Hospitable.pdf. Internet. Accessed on 18 April 2006.

Blanchard, Christopher M. 2005. *Al Qaeda: Statements and evolving ideology.* Washington, DC: Library of Congress.

Booker, Salih, and Ann-Louise Colgan. 2006. Africa Policy Outlook. *Foreign policy in focus.* Available from http://www.fpif.org/fpiftxt/3157. Internet. Accessed on 6 May 2006

Botha, Anneli. 2005. *Terrorism in Africa.* Pretoria South Africa: Centre for International Political Studies.

Botha, Anneli, and Hussein Solomon. 2005. Terrorism in Africa. Ph.D. diss., Centre for International Political Studies.

Brachman, Jarret M., and William F. McCants. 2006. *Stealing Al-Qa'ida's playbook.* West Point, NY: Counter Terrorism Center.

Bumiller, Elisabeth. 2005. White House letter: 21st-century warnings of a threat rooted in the 7th century. *New York Times*, 12 December.

Chalk, Peter. 2003. Countering Nigerian organized crime. *Jane's Intelligence Review* (September): 1-4.

Corey, Charles W. 2004. *US helping Africa win its fight against terrorism.* Available from http://www.globalsecurity.org/security/library/news/2004/10/sec-041021-usia03.htm. Internet. Accessed on 22 September 2005.

Congressional Research Service. 2006. Available from http://www.loc.gov/crsinfo/whatscrs.html. Internet. Accessed on 18 April 2006.

Dickson, David. 2005. *Political Islam in Sub-Saharan Africa: The need for new research and diplomatic agenda.* US Institute of Peace, Special Report. Available from http://www.usip.org/pubs/special reports/sr140.html. Internet. Accessed on 18 October 2005.

eia.doe.gov. 2005. Nigeria country brief analysis. Washington DC: Department of Energy. Database on-line. Available from http://www.eia.doe.gove/emeu/cabs/nigeria.html. Internet. Accessed on 18 April 2006.

Emerson, Steven. 2003. Third public hearing of the National Commission on terrorist attacks upon the US, 9 July. Available from http://www.9-11commission.gov/hearings/hearings3/witness_emerson.htm. Internet. Accessed on 18 April 2006.

Esposito, John L. 1999. *The Islamic threat myth or reality.* New York: Oxford University Press.

Farah, Douglas. 2003. *Blood from stones: The secret financial network of terror.* New York, NY: Broadway Books.

_____. 2004a. *Debate over Al Qaeda's connection to West Africa's diamond trade.* Available from http://allafrica.com/stories/200408050800.html. Internet. Accessed on 22 September 2005.

_____. 2004b. *Blood from stones: The secret financial network of terror.* New York: Random House, Inc.

Foreign Broadcast Information Service. 2005. Lagos Weekend Vanguard. Available from http://www.vanguardngr.com/vag.htm. Internet. Accessed on 18 October 2005.

Freidman, Thomas L. 2005. *The world is flat: A brief history of the twenty first century.* New York: Farrar, Straus and Giroux.

Glazov, Jamie. 2005. Sharia goes global. Interview with Paul Marshall. Available from http://www.frontpagemag.com/Articles/ReadArticle.asp?ID=19670. Internet. Accessed on 18 April 2006.

Globalsecurity.org. 2006. Available from http://www.globalsecurity.org/military/ops/pan-sahel.htm. Internet. Accessed on 5 May 2006.

Gunaratna, Rohan. 2002. *Inside Al Qaeda.* New York, NY: The Berkley Publishing Group.

Harmony Database. 2006. Al-Qa'ida constitutional charter. West Point, NY: Counter Terrorism Center. Available at http://www.ctc.usma.edu/harmony_docs.asp. Internet. Accessed on 17 March 2006.

Henderson, Simon. 2003. Institutionalized Islam: Saudi Arabia's Islamic policies and the threat they pose. Testimony, US Senate Committee on the Judiciary Terrorism: Two Years After 9/11, Connecting the Dots. Available from http://judiciary.senate.gov/testimony.cfm?id=910&wit_id=2573. Internet. Accessed on 18 April 2006.

Huntington, Samuel P. 1996. *The clash of civilizations and the remaking of world order.* New York, NY: Simon and Schuster.

International Crisis Group Africa. 2005. *Islamist terrorism in the Sahel: Fact or fiction?* Report N 92, 31 March. Available from http://www.crisisgroup.org/home/index.cfm?l=1&id=3349. Internet. Accessed on 18 April 2006.

IRINnews.org. 2004. Nigeria: Muslim fundamentalist uprising raises fears of terrorism. Available from http://www.irinnews.org/S_report.asp?ReportID=39110&SelectRegion=West_Africa. Internet. Accessed on 29 September 2005.

Islam On-line. 2006. Available from http://www.islamonline.com. Internet. Accessed on 22 February 2006.

Joint Chiefs of Staff. 2006. *National military strategic plan for the war on terrorism.* Washington, DC: Department of Defense.

Kaplan, David E., Monica Ekman, and Aamir Latif. 2003. How billions in oil money spawned a global terror network. *U.S. News & World Report* (15 December): 1. Available from http://www.usnews.com/usnews/news/articles/031215/15terror.htm. Internet. Accessed 18 April 2006.

Kaplan Robert D. 2005. *Imperial grunts: The American military on the ground.* New York: Random House.

Kurz, Anat, and Nahman Tal. 1997. *Hamas: Radical Islam in a national struggle*. Memorandum No. 48. Tel Aviv University Jaffee Center for Strategic Studies. Available from http://www.tau.ac.il/jcss/memoranda/m48chp4.html. Internet. Accessed on 7 May 2006.

Laremont, Ricardo, Ph.D., and Hrach Gregorian, Ph. D. 2006. Political Islam in West Africa and the Sahel. *Military Review* (January February): 36.

Laqueur Walter. 2004. *No end to war: Terrorism in the twenty first century*. New York, NY: The Continuum International Publishing Group.

Lewis, Bernard. 2003. *The crisis of Islam: Holy war and unholy terror*. New York, NY: Random House.

Lewis, Peter. 2004. Radio Netherlands. Radio interview transcripts with Netherlands, Professor Peter Lewis, an expert on Nigerian affairs with the Council on International Relations in Washington. Available from http://www2.rnw.nl/ rnw/en/currentaffairs/region/africa/nig040924.html. Internet. Accessed on 29 September 2005.

Mair, Stefan. 2003. Terrorism and Africa on the danger of further attacks in sub-Saharan Africa. *African Security Review* 12, no 1: 1.

Marshall, Paul. 2004. Outside encouragement Sharia rules Nigeria, with the help of foreign Islamists. *National Review Online*. Available from http://www.nation alreview.com/ comment/marshall200405050847.asp. Internet. Accessed on 18 April 2006.

Mazel, Zvi. 2005. How Egypt molded modern radical Islam. *Jerusalem Center for Public Affairs, Jerusalem Issue Brief* 4, no. 18 (February). Available from http://www. jcpa.org/brief/brief004-18.htm. Internet. Accessed on 18 April 2006.

McCormack, David. 2005. African vortex: Islamism in Sub-Saharan Africa. *Center for Security Policy, Occasional Paper Series* 4. Washington, DC: Government Printing Office. Available from http://www.centerforsecuritypolicy.org/ Af_Vortex.pdf. Internet. Accessed on 18 April 2006.

Miko, Francis T. 2004. *Removing terrorist sanctuaries: The 9/11 commission recommendations and U.S policy*. Washington, DC: Congressional Research Service, Library of Congress.

National Intelligence Council. 2004. *Mapping the global future: Report of the national intelligence council's 2020 project*. Washington, DC: Government Printing Office. GPO stock number 041-015-00240-6.

Oysanya, Femi. 2004. Nigeria: Haven for terrorist internet communications? Article online. Available from http://www.nigeriavillagesquare1.com/Articles/femi_oyesanya/oyesanya.html. Internet. Accessed on 8 March 2006.

Rabasa, Angel M., Peter Chalk, Ian Lesser, David Thaler, Rollie Lal, Christine Fair, Theodore Karaski, and Cheryl Benard. 2004. *The Muslim world after 9/11*. Santa Monica, CA: RAND Corporation.

Real Instituto Elcano de Estudios Internacionalies y Estrategicos. 2005. The London bombings and the broader strategic context (ARI). Available from http://www.realinstitut oelcano.org/analisis/787.asp. Internet. Accessed on 18 April 2006.

Sageman, Marc. 2004. *Understanding terror networks*. Philadelphia, PA: University Pennsylvania Press.

Saudi Arabian Information Resource. 2006. Available from http://www.saudinf.com/main/c6e.htm. Internet. Accessed on 17 January 2006.

Schwartz Stephen. 2005. *Naming names: A GAO report unabashedly names America's foe in the war on terrorism, Islamic extremism.* Available from http://www.weeklystandard.com/Content/Public/Articles/000/000/006/107rbmev.asp. Internet. Accessed on 21 September 2005.

Shultz, Richard H., Douglas Farah, and Itamara V. Lochard. 2004. *Armed groups: A tier-one security priority*. INSS Occasional Paper 57 (September). USAF Academy, CO: USAF Institute for National Security Studies

Spencer, Robert. 2002. *Islam unveiled, disturbing questions about the world's fastest-growing faith.* San Francisco: Encounter Books.

The White House. 2002. *The national security strategy of the US of America.* Washington, DC: Government Printing Office

_____. 2003. *National military strategy for combating terrorism.* Washington, DC. Available from http://www.whitehouse.gov/news/releases/2003/02/counter_terrorism/counter_terrorism_strategy.pdf. Internet. Accessed on 18 April 2006.

_____. 2006. President Bush gives state of the union address. Washington, DC. Available from http://www.whitehouse.gov/news/releases/2006/01/ 20060131-10.html. Internet. Accessed on 18 April 2006.

Trifkovic, Serge. 2002. *The sword of the Prophet Islam history, theology, impact on the world.* Boston, MA: Regina Orthodox Press, Inc.

Ye'or, Bat. 2005. *Eurabia The Euro-Arab Axis: Land of Dhimmitude Eurabia Land of Islams*. Cranbury, NJ: Associated University Presses.